WITHDRAWN

73213
5.99
J 338.4
Fre

VIP*
who work with
RECREATION VEHICLES

by
Freeman, Westover, and Willis
Illustrated by Harry Garo

* **Very Important People Series**

AN ELK GROVE BOOK

 CHILDRENS PRESS, CHICAGO

UNIVERSITY SCHOOL LIBRARY
UNIVERSITY OF WYOMING

Library of Congress Cataloging in Publication Data

Freeman, Dorothy Rhodes.
   Very important people who work with recreation
vehicles.

   (VIP series, set I. The work world of wheels,
book 3)
   SUMMARY: Discusses the jobs of people who make,
sell, repair, and deal in other ways with bicycles,
motorcycles, snowmobiles, campers, and other
recreational vehicles.

   "An Elk Grove book."

   1. Automobile industry and trade—Vocational
guidance—Juvenile literature. 2. Motor vehicles—
Recreational use—Juvenile literature. [1. Automobile
industry and trade—Vocational guidance. 2. Motor
vehicles—Recreational use] I. Westover, Margaret,
joint author. II. Willis, Willma, joint author.
III. Garo, Harry, illus. IV. Title. V. Title:
Recreation vehicles.
TL147.F74   338.4'7'6292023   72-10385
ISBN 0-516-07452-0

Copyright © 1973 Regensteiner Publishing Enterprises, Inc.
All rights reserved. Published simultaneously in Canada.
Printed in the United States of America.

1 2 3 4 5 6 7 8 9 10 11 12 13 14 15 16 17 18 19 20 21 22 23 24 25 R 75 74 73

VIP*
who work with
RECREATION VEHICLES

SET 1 - BOOK 3

* **Very Important People Series**

V.I.P. SERIES

CONTENTS

If you work with RECREATION VEHICLES, you could be . . .

A WAREHOUSE MANAGER

A CABINET MAKER

AN UPHOLSTERER

A FORK LIFT OPERATOR

A SNOW SURVEYOR

A WHEEL LACER

A MOTORCYCLE
MECHANIC

A WELDER

A MOTORCYCLE PARTS SALESMAN

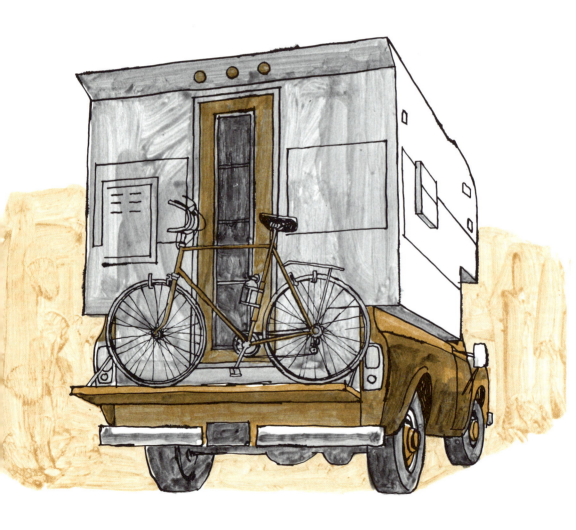

VEHICLES FOR FUN

Vehicles for fun—recreation vehicles—are in!

Bicycles, minibikes, motorcycles, snowmobiles, dune cycles, campers, trailers, motorhomes—these are just some of the vehicles people use for fun and hobbies.

Recreation vehicles are called *RV's* for short.

Many people travel with their families in *motorhomes* and *campers*. Look what's fastened on behind! Bicycles, motorcycles, and even *4WD's*.

When they park at campgrounds, these people use the extra vehicles they bring along to explore off the main roads. They ride mountain trails, travel over deserts and sand dunes, and have a wonderful time.

CHOOSING YOUR WORK

There are few jobs for drivers of recreation vehicles, but lots of workers are needed to design, build, and service them. Other people can find work at the parks where RV owners go to camp and ride the trails.

You need to figure out some of your interests and skills to know which RV jobs may be right for you.

On the next page are three sets of questions to help you.

1. Do you like to work with your hands and tools? Do you like to take mechanical things apart to see how they are put together? Have you ever bought tools for yourself? Do you like to get tools as presents? Do you look at the engine on a motorcycle before you look at the fancy trim?
2. Do you like to work with numbers and lists? Do you like to follow the directions to make models from a kit? Do you like to compare the facts about different makes of bikes? Do you like to keep lists of race winners?
3. Do you like to work with people? Do you like to join clubs? Do you spend a lot of time talking with friends and discussing hobbies?

Which set of questions made you feel like answering "yes"? Are you one of the people who are most interested in working with

1. hands
You might assemble or repair recreation vehicles.

2. numbers and lists
You might design or plan changes for these vehicles. You might keep records for a dealer.

3. people?
You might enjoy selling RV's or working at a recreation vehicle park.

This book is about all these and other Very Important People (V.I.P.) who work in the world of recreation vehicles.

Watch for the symbols, , , and to help you see how the jobs fit your skills and interests. When you see more than one symbol, the first one is more important than the ones that follow.

V.I.P. WHO WORK WITH BICYCLES

Bicycles are very popular.

Many people use them for cheap transportation to work or school and for fun and exercise. A few people ride them while they're working. Perhaps you have used a bike to deliver papers or do errands.

Most jobs for people who work with bicycles are in the factories where bicycles are made.

In one large U.S. manufacturing plant, 1,700 workers, doing many different jobs, make 5,600 bicycles each working day. Some workers make the parts, then others put all the parts together to complete the bicycles.

PEOPLE WHO MAKE BICYCLE PARTS

BRAZERS and **WELDERS** join pieces of steel tubing to make the bicycle *frames* and *wheel forks*. These workers use *acetylene torches* or *electric arc* welders.

Brazers need less training and experience than welders.

MACHINE OPERATORS make the bicycle fenders. They feed *strip steel* into automatic forming machines, and the fenders come out of the machine ready for paint.

Frames, forks, and fenders travel on a *conveyor* into a painting booth. An operator controls the paint spraying machine. The painted parts are then dried in rooms that are kept at an even temperature.

Another worker called a **LACER** gets the wheels ready. He puts the *spokes* in the wheels. Then he fastens each spoke to the rim by tightening a small nut.

15

PEOPLE WHO ASSEMBLE BICYCLES

 BENCH ASSEMBLERS sit or stand at benches where they put many small pieces together to make hand brakes, gear changers, and other *sub-assemblies.*

In a large manufacturing plant, sub-assemblies and other parts are put on hooks on an overhead conveyor that travels through the factory.

LINE ASSEMBLERS work beside a slowly-moving platform. The bicycle frames are fastened upside down on the platform. Each line assembler reaches up and takes a part off the overhead conveyor. He fastens the part to the bicycle frame.

At the end of the assembly line, workers drop a cardboard carton over the bicycle. Into the carton they also put packages that contain handlebars, pedals, seat, nuts and bolts, and the directions for completing the assembly.

A few expensive bikes, such as racers, are completed in the factory. Workers who specialize in assembling these make sure that all parts fit and work perfectly. This *custom assembly* takes more time and skill than line assembly, and it makes these bikes cost more than line-assembled bikes.

INSPECTORS check all the materials and parts throughout the factory. They make sure that each bicycle is made according to the standards set by the manufacturer.

Who can work in a bicycle factory? The people in charge of one of the largest bicycle manufacturing companies say they want men or women who

- are dependable and can get to the job on time each day
- like to work with their hands and use tools
- can listen to directions and learn by watching others.

Employers like to hire workers who have finished high school.

Experienced workers train newcomers who show they are willing to listen and learn.

PEOPLE WHO STORE BICYCLES

Work with bicycles doesn't end when the bicycle goes into its carton.

FORK LIFT OPERATORS take the stacks of boxed bicycles to trucks that haul the load to a warehouse.

The **WAREHOUSE MANAGER** keeps records to show how many bicycles he has stored. **WAREHOUSE WORKERS** must be able to read and understand the *stock numbers* on the cartons. They organize the cartons so they can fill orders quickly, according to the model and color wanted.

PEOPLE WHO DISTRIBUTE BICYCLES

A **DISTRIBUTOR** buys many bicycles from several man-ufacturers and stores them in warehouses in different parts of the country.

The **BICYCLE DEALER** orders the bicycles he needs from the distributor and sells them in his store. He hires salesmen and mechanics to help him.

People who want bicycles often depend upon a **SALESMAN** for advice. A good bicycle salesman

- knows how to operate all kinds of bicycles
- knows which features of the bicycle are important to the customer
- knows where to find parts and accessories in the store
- is able to write receipts for money and can order parts
- can keep the showroom neat and attractive.

Some dealers say they like to hire young people who are members of bicycle riding or racing clubs. They figure that these people are really interested in bicycles, and that their friends may become customers.

PEOPLE WHO REPAIR
AND ASSEMBLE BICYCLES

When the bicycles are delivered to the dealer, a **ME-CHANIC** puts them together and adjusts them. He fastens the handlebars to the frame, fits the wheels into the forks, and fastens the seat in place.

A dealer may hire several mechanics. Each mechanic has his own *station,* the place where he does his work. He provides his own tools. He may specialize in assembling bikes that come from the warehouse, or he may repair wheels and spokes, adjust gears, handbrakes, coaster brakes, and other systems.

Who can be a bicycle mechanic? Young men and women who

- like to work with their hands
- like to use tools
- are dependable
- have some experience working on bicycles.

PEOPLE WHO RENT BICYCLES

In nearly every large recreation area, such as the national parks, you can find a sign that says "Bicycles for Rent."

Young people with skill in bicycle maintenance can get jobs renting and repairing bicycles.

They adjust brakes, seats, and gears, patch bicycle tubes, and tighten spokes. Other jobs they do are filling out forms and collecting rental fees. They need to enjoy serving people.

PEOPLE WHO
MANUFACTURE BICYCLE ACCESSORIES

Accessories are extra equipment or parts that add to the rider's comfort and safety.

Some companies make headlights, radios, horns, baskets, carrying racks, and locks. One company manufactures a rack that holds a surfboard on a bike.

Another company specializes in racks to park bikes and racks to carry them on cars.

Many different workers help design, manufacture, and sell these accessories.

Employees say they hire both men and women over 18 years old. No special training is required, but skill in working with tools is helpful.

Most accessory manufacturing companies will train an interested person who wants to learn.

V.I.P. WHO WORK WITH MOTORCYCLES

Motorcycles are exciting machines. More than three million owners ride them to work, to school, for traveling, exploring, racing, and stunting.

There aren't many jobs for people who ride motorcycles as part of their work. A few, such as police officers and some deliverymen, ride motorcycles on their jobs.

There aren't many motorcycle manufacturing jobs in the U.S., because most motorcycles are manufactured in Japan, France, Germany, England, and Italy. There is only one manufacturer of motorcycles in the U.S.A.

But if you like to be around motorcycles, there are many jobs selling and repairing them.

PEOPLE WHO SELL MOTORCYCLES

Each factory that makes motorcycles has salesmen in the United States. Salesmen from the factories are called **MANUFACTURING REPRESENTATIVES.** They know all about the latest models. Sometimes they give special classes so that other salesmen can learn about the changes that are made each year.

The manufacturing representative may sell the motorcycles to another salesman called a **DISTRIBUTOR.** The distributor then sells to the store owner.

A distributor usually buys from different manufacturing representatives so he can offer several makes of motorcycles to the store owners.

The motorcycles are kept in warehouses in crates until the dealer needs them. A **WAREHOUSE MANAGER** keeps records to show where each brand and model is stored. His **FORK LIFT OPERATORS** go to the right storage place and take the crated cycles to a truck that hauls them to the store owner.

The store owner is called a **DEALER.** He displays different makes of motorcycles in his showroom. He hires **SALESMEN** to help customers and to advise them about which model to buy.

The dealer often sells used motorcycles as well as new ones.

Many motorcycle owners repair their own machines or make changes on them. The owners buy the parts from a **PARTS SALESMAN** at the dealer's shop.

A parts salesman has to know all the latest changes in motorcycles. He reads catalogs and parts lists carefully. He understands stock numbers that tell him where to find a part on his shelves. If his department doesn't have the part, he orders it from a manufacturer.

Some women and girls, who ride motorcycles and know a lot about them, find jobs managing or helping in parts departments.

PEOPLE WHO REPAIR MOTORCYCLES

A motorcycle needs good care to be dependable.

Some owners are able to do most of the repairs on their motorcycles, but thousands of others depend on a **MOTORCYCLE MECHANIC.**

It may seem strange, but many people who buy motorcycles don't even know how to ride them. They haven't any idea how to do *routine maintenance* or repair. Some owners need help for such simple things as tightening a chain or changing a spark plug.

Most motorcycle mechanics work in shops owned by dealers.

Before the mechanic begins his work, a **SERVICE MANAGER** talks to the customer and writes a *shop order* that lists the problems and the needed repairs.

The mechanic repairs the engine and *transmission,* does electrical work, and adjusts and repairs brakes. He *lubricates* the parts. He changes or tightens spokes and repairs tires. He may do frame and fork straightening.

Most experienced mechanics know how to do all these jobs, but in large shops, a mechanic may specialize in only one or two jobs.

A mechanic uses many different tools. A *strobe light* helps him check the *timing* of an engine. An *exhaust analyzer* tells him if *cylinders* are leaking and if fuel is burning properly.

For some repairs the mechanic may use a *drill press,* a *brake-drum lathe,* or a machine for *reboring* cylinders.

These tools usually belong to the repair shop.

Mechanics may have their own set of hand tools, too. Beginners start with a simple tool kit and add to it as they learn and earn more money.

If you are pretty good at fixing your own bicycle or minibike, you probably could learn to be a motorcycle mechanic.

How do you get started in motorcycle repair?

Find out where the repairing is done near your home. (Look in the Yellow Pages of the telephone book.) Most of the work is done in small shops, so you might get a chance to talk to a mechanic and learn from him.

Library books and motorcycle magazines can also help you learn.

In some high school shop classes you can learn repair and maintenance of *four-cycle* and *two-cycle* engines that power motorcycles.

Manufacturers of motorcycles sometimes hold training

classes to teach mechanics what they need to know about repairing their latest models.

Motorcycle mechanics can repair small engines in other machines, such as snowmobiles, power lawn mowers, and small boats.

Mechanics who are able to work well with people, as well as with tools, may become service managers.

Those who specialize in one make of motorcycle may become manufacturing representatives.

Who can be a motorcycle mechanic? One who

- likes to work with small engines and is skilled in using tools
- is able to follow printed instructions
- doesn't mind the noise of loud engines
- is neat and careful and able to keep his tools and jobs organized
- is willing to study to keep up with the latest model changes.

Motorcycle riders often want to change or modify their motorcycles. If they are good mechanics, they can make their own changes. Sometimes they need help to plan the changes or to complete the job.

CUSTOM MECHANICS, working in *custom design shops,* specialize in designing and rebuilding motorcycles to suit their customers.

The custom design shop is an interesting place to work if you like to dream up and test new ideas.

PEOPLE WHO MAKE MOTORCYCLE PARTS

Many motorcycle jobs are with companies that make special parts. These parts improve the motorcycle's performance, appearance, or safety.

One such company makes shock absorbers that improve the ride and make bumps and jolts easier on the rider. Another makes replacement forks, frames, and fuel tanks.

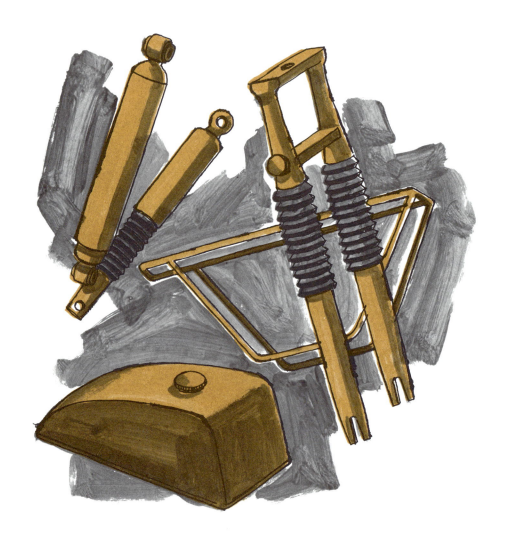

PEOPLE WHO MAKE MOTORCYCLE ACCESSORIES

Accessories are extra equipment for the motorcycle or the rider.

The motorcyclist's most important accessory is his *safety helmet*. Riders call them "skid lids" or "brain buckets." Some state laws say that all motorcycle riders must wear helmets. All recreation and racing tracks require them.

Helmets are made by manufacturers who specialize in making plastic or *fiberglass* accessories.

A *fairing* is a fiberglass accessory. It fits on the handlebars of the motorcycle and holds the windshield. The fairing and the windshield protect the rider from the wind.

Saddlebags are cargo carriers that fasten on both sides of the rear wheel. These and other larger cargo carriers are made of fiberglass, leather, tough plastics, or metal.

Motorcycle riders who race or drive off the highways often damage the metal fenders of their bikes. A plastics manufacturer designed a fender that will bend double without breaking. Motorcycle dealers sell these plastic fenders in many different colors to match and fit almost any make of bike.

Off-road riders and racers need special protective clothing. Heavy trousers, called leathers, gloves, boots, padded vests and heavy jackets are some of the important accessories for these riders.

Workers who make these accessories get their training on the job. Young people can learn to do fiberglass work quickly. They learn to operate large sewing machines and to assemble and package the accessories.

Students in high school *work experience programs* can get school credit while working part time on some of these accessory manufacturing jobs.

V.I.P. WHO WORK WITH SNOWMOBILES

Over two million snowmobiles roar across streets and trails in the snow country of the United States and Canada.

These motor-driven sleds provide fun for their owners and jobs for the people who build and service them.

Snowmobiles are operated by two-cycle engines. The engine turns a continuous *drive track* that makes the sled move. The driver guides it with handlebars that turn the ski-like runners.

Snowmobiles are made in large factories in Canada and the U.S. Jobs in these factories are assembly line jobs. Most of the **ASSEMBLERS** learn on the job.

DESIGNERS and manufacturers try to make snowmobiles safer and quieter. The latest snowmobiles have *disc brakes* for faster stops, crash padded handlebars, and safety guards for moving parts.

Some manufacturers set up *safety clinics* that are held at snowmobile dealers .

36

The **DEALER** orders from the factories and sells to the customer. He teaches customers how to operate the snowmobiles. Mechanics in the dealer's garage service and repair snowmobiles.

A **SNOWMOBILE MECHANIC** has the same skills as a motorcycle mechanic. He has to be an expert in the repair and adjustment of two-cycle engines. In addition, he must be willing to live in snow country.

In most snow resort areas, you can find snowmobiles for rent. There are jobs in resorts for workers who can get along well with people, service and maintain the rental snowmobiles, and keep good records.

A few people use snowmobiles as transportation on their jobs.

SNOW SURVEYORS use them as they travel into the mountains to measure the snowfall. This information helps them to forecast the future water supply.

Some **GAME WARDENS,** who work in wilderness areas, travel on snowmobiles.

Farmers use snowmobiles to get feed to stranded cattle in the winter.

Sheriffs' rescue teams use them to search for people stranded in the snow.

V.I.P. WHO WORK WITH SHELTERS ON WHEELS

On weekends and holidays, drivers of recreation vehicles head for campgrounds and other recreation areas. Many of them drive or pull a home on wheels. It may be a motorhome, travel trailer, camper, or van.

Because of all these RV's, there are many jobs for designers, draftsmen, welders, carpenters, electricians, upholsterers, and cabinet makers.

PEOPLE WHO BUILD MOTORHOMES

The name, motorhome, is a good description of the vehicle. It is like a small house and is built on a special *chassis.*

The motorhome manufacturer buys the chassis from a truck manufacturer. It comes with a basic engine attached to a steel frame on wheels.

It rolls in one end of the factory at the start of the production line. A finished, ready-to-use motorhome is driven out of the factory at the other end of the line.

A **MECHANIC** is the first person to work on the chassis.
He services the engine, making sure that the plugs are firing
right. He checks the transmission oil and adjusts the carbu-
retor and the timing. If the customer has ordered special
equipment, he installs it. This could be an air conditioner,
a *transmission cooler,* special tires, or other custom items.

Next, a **WELDER** adds metal crossbars to the chassis to support the floor.

The chassis rolls to the next work station where a **CAR-PENTER** builds a floor on top of the metal crossbars.

An **ELECTRICIAN** installs wires for headlights, rear lights, and living quarters.

A **CARPET LAYER** installs thick carpet.

The V.I.P. who knows how to do all these jobs is the **LEADMAN**. One leadman supervises several work stations. He walks from station to station along the production line, making sure that all the work is going OK. Sometimes he picks up a tool and helps. He trains new men who come to the job.

In the factory *woodshop,* carpenters called **CABINET MAKERS** build the cupboards that go into the motorhomes.

The **MILLMAN** cuts the lumber, then the cabinet makers assemble, sand, and stain the cabinets. They also make the frames for the couches and dinettes.

Both men and women work in the woodshop.

UPHOLSTERERS add the padding and covers to the dinette benches and the couches. They make patterns, fit, cut, and sew fabrics and plastics.

The **TRIMMERS** work with the upholsterers. They add foam rubber padding and springs.

Upholsterers use scissors, knives, *power staplers,* and wrenches. With electric steaming machines they shrink or stretch fabrics to improve the fit. With *heat welders* they bind synthetic fabrics together.

After most of the furniture and cabinets are in, **FINISH-ERS** install the *appliances*. These small sinks, stoves, and refrigerators are made in other factories and bought by the motorhome manufacturer.

The next big job is to add the sides and roof to the vehicle. These are usually made by another manufacturer and shipped to the motorhome factory in *panels*. Panels are entire outside walls.

After these are installed, other finishers put in window frames and glass.

They add other finishing items like light fixtures, cabinet handles and curtains.

Now the motorhome is ready to roll!

INSPECTORS do the final work before the motorhome is ready to sell. One inspector takes each motorhome for a test run. He listens for unusual noises in the engine or other parts.

The highest paid factory worker is the **TROUBLE-SHOOTER**. He repairs or changes anything the inspectors find wrong. Troubleshooters are V.I.P. because they know how to take apart and repair all mechanical parts of the engine and interior parts of the home.

About 35 people work on each motorhome.

Owners and managers of motorhome factories say they want employees who are

- able to learn from a more experienced worker
- willing to listen to directions
- able to get along with other people.

Most employers think that these traits are more important than the length of a person's hair, his education, or previous experience. They look especially for men and women who want to learn. They encourage a worker to advance to leadman or even factory manager.

PEOPLE WHO BUILD CAMPERS

Campers are living quarters made to fit on the back of *pick-up trucks*.

The framework of the camper is called a *shell*. After the shell is finished, the interior is finished and furnished. Some small campers have sleeping space only. A larger one may have beds, a kitchen, and sometimes a bathroom.

CARPENTERS and **UPHOLSTERERS** are the V.I.P. who do most of the work on campers.

Some factories buy and complete camper shells and furnish the inside.

It doesn't take much room or equipment to make a camper shell. Two or three ambitious people with carpentry skills can build camper shells in a small work space such as a garage or store building.

PEOPLE WHO BUILD TRAVEL TRAILERS

Travel trailers have no engine and are towed by a car or truck. Inside and outside they are a lot like the living quarters of a motorhome.

 The people who build them are **CARPENTERS**, **UPHOL-STERERS**, and **ELECTRICIANS**.

PEOPLE WHO CONVERT VANS

A *van* is a vehicle with a large, enclosed body, an engine, and space for the driver. Vans were originally designed for delivery men to use.

After young people discovered how useful vans can be, *van conversion companies* began to furnish the interiors with many comforts.

The conversion companies buy the vans with nothing inside except engines and the drivers' seats. Workers replace the van top with a raised section so people can stand up inside. They cut holes for windows and install frames and glass. They add appliances, beds, seats, and even bathroom fixtures.

For customers who are surfers, the van conversion companies make a special model. They pad the interior with thick carpeting and install a stereo unit and speakers.

CARPENTERS, UPHOLSTERERS, and **FINISHERS** do the van conversions.

Many salesmen are needed to sell trailers, vans, campers, and motorhomes. They sell for **DEALERS** who specialize in one or more of these RV's. Some automobile dealers also sell RV's.

Vans and motorhomes need repair and maintenance on their engines. **MECHANICS** at dealers' or general repair garages do these services.

PEOPLE WHO WORK AT RV PARKS

So many people are touring in their RV's that public parks are running out of overnight parking spaces for them.

Businessmen who know about this problem build RV parks. These overnight stopping places offer more than sleeping space. Some have swimming pools, miniature golf courses, picnic areas, and playgrounds. They have laundry rooms and small stores.

Some of the park jobs are maintaining the park grounds and working in the park store. In parks that have stables, there are jobs caring for horses.

GENERAL STORE

V.I.P. WHO WORK WITH FOUR-WHEEL-DRIVE VEHICLES

The most unusual work with a *four-wheeler* is for **AS-TRONAUTS** who drive a lunar rover while they are exploring the moon.

There aren't many jobs for "moon buggy" drivers, but there are many jobs for people who like to work with "earth rovers."

Four-wheelers are four-wheel-drive vehicles called "4-WD" or "4x4" for short. The transmission supplies power to all four wheels. If one wheel gets stuck in mud or sand, the other wheels have power to move the 4-WD.

FOREST RANGERS patrol mountain roads and trails in 4WD vehicles. Rescue workers, searching for lost people in rugged country, use them.

There are jobs in manufacturing, repairing, and selling 4-WD's.

These vehicles are manufactured in factories where many people are employed. Some jobs are for **DESIGNERS, DRAFTSMEN, MACHINISTS, ASSEMBLERS,** and **INSPECTORS.***

Some factories employ people to build accessories such as *heavy-duty bumpers, tow bars,* and *winches.* A winch is a drum-shaped wheel, wound with a strong rope or cable. One end of the rope can be fastened to a tree or post. Using its own engine to turn the wheel, the 4-WD can pull itself out of mud or sand.

Manufacturers like to hire workers who

- like to work with their hands and tools
- are willing to learn and can follow directions
- have some skills in working with metals.

*These jobs are explained in Book I of the V.I.P. Series, **V.I.P. WHO WORK WITH CARS, BUSES, AND TRUCKS.**

V.I.P. WHO WORK WITH MINIBIKES, GO-KARTS, AND OTHER RV'S

There are some RV's that can't be licensed for street travel, but are made for trail riding.

They are made just for recreation. The jobs with them are in assembling, selling, and servicing.

A minibike has a gasoline engine and two small wheels with large rubber tires. Most minibikes are imported. A few are assembled from imported parts.

U.S. factories build a bike called a trail bike. It's heavier and larger than a minibike. One worker assembles a complete bike.

Go-karts are small, four-wheeled vehicles that are usually driven on tracks made especially for them. There are jobs assembling them and running the parks.

A few go-karts are used by driver training teachers.

V.I.P. WHO OPERATE
OFF-ROAD VEHICLE PARKS

 Owners of minibikes, trail bikes, and motorcycles who want to explore or climb hills don't have many places to ride.

Before there were so many of these RV's, their owners could ride on vacant land. However, as their numbers increased, a problem grew. Residents near the vacant land and campers in parks complained about noise. Farmers complained about the erosion and dust.

The *Federal Bureau of Land Management,* cooperating with RV clubs, began to plan areas where off-road vehicle drivers could enjoy riding on public lands.

Businessmen started to operate special parks with trails for riding and sometimes spaces for camping.

There are some jobs for young people in these parks.

V.I.P. WHO WRITE ABOUT RECREATION VEHICLES

There is a lot of material written about motorcycles, bicycles, snowmobiles, motorhomes, campers, and trailers. Most newspapers have articles about them and over a hundred magazines specialize in articles about them.

Young **WRITERS** who know a lot about RV's can try to have their writing published. Most magazines and newspapers pay for articles and for photographs. Some pay for ideas and suggestions.

Before you send articles to any publications, read them carefully to give you an idea of the type of writing they prefer. You can get copies at libraries and at news stands.

Your school librarian or English teacher can help you find out how to submit articles and pictures.

RV'S IN YOUR FUTURE

Fun with recreation vehicles is contagious. Friends tell other friends and fads start! Many families enjoy RV's together.

People with good imaginations design new RV's. Some recent ones are the three-wheel dune cycle and the *all-terrain vehicle*.

The more RV's, the more jobs there are for people who build, repair, and sell them. Parks for RV's will continue to need more workers.

Here is a field where hobbies can turn into jobs. The information a young person gets repairing and taking care of his or his friend's RV's can get him started working with them.

Employers in most factories are willing to let dependable young people learn as they earn.

GLOSSARY/INDEX

Note Some of the words defined in this glossary have several meanings. The meanings described here are the ones used in this book.

60

Federal Bureau of
Land Management, 56 a government agency in charge of the
use of public land

fiberglass, 34 a material made of fine strands of

finisher, 46, 51 a worker who does the final jobs

forest ranger, 54 a person who supervises the use and
care of a forest

fork-lift
operator, 19, 26 the operator of a vehicle used for
lifting and moving large, heavy
objects

four-cycle, 29 an engine in which each cylinder
delivers power at every other
revolution of the engine

four-wheeler, 53 a four-wheel drive vehicle

4 W D, 9 same as a four-wheeler

frame, 13 the part of a bicycle or other vehicle
to which most other parts are
attached

game warden, 37 a government worker who sees that
hunting and fishing laws are obeyed

heat welder, 45 a machine that fastens together
plastics and other synthetic materials
by means of heat

heavy duty
bumper, 54 an extra strong bumper

inspector, 18, 47, 54 a person who checks the quality of
materials and products

lacer, 15 a worker who inserts and adjusts the
spokes in wheels

leadman, 42 a person who supervises other
workers

line assembler, 17 a worker who attaches parts to a
vehicle as it goes past on a moving
platform

lubricate, 29 apply oil or grease to machinery parts